D1300328

ENCOUNTERING
GHOSTS

EYEWITNESS ACCOUNTS

by Mari Bolte

illustrated by Kako

Consultant:
Jerome Clark
J. Allen Hynek Center for UFO Studies
Chicago, Illinois

CAPSTONE PRESS
a capstone imprint

Graphic Library is published by Capstone Press,
1710 Roe Crest Drive, North Mankato, Minnesota 56003
www.capstonepub.com

Copyright © 2015 by Capstone Press, a Capstone imprint. All rights reserved. No part of
this publication may be reproduced in whole or in part, or stored in a retrieval system, or
transmitted in any form or by any means, electronic, mechanical, photocopying, recording,
or otherwise, without written permission of the publisher.

Library of Congress Cataloging-in-Publication Data
Cataloging-in-publication information is on file with the Library of Congress.
Bolte, Mari., author.
  Encountering ghosts : eyewitness accounts / by Mari Bolte ; illustrated by Kako.
    pages cm.—(Graphic library. Eyewitness to the unexplained)
  Summary: "Stories of ghost encounters are told using eyewitness accounts in graphic
novel format"—Provided by publisher.
  Audience: 8-14.
  Audience: Grades 4 to 6.
  Includes bibliographical references and index.
  ISBN 978-1-4914-0245-0 (library binding)
  ISBN 978-1-4914-0250-4 (ebook pdf)
1. Ghosts—Juvenile literature. 2. Ghosts—Comic books, strips, etc. 3. Apparitions—
Juvenile literature. 4. Apparitions—Comic books, strips, etc. I. Kako, 1975– illustrator.
II. Title.
  BF1461.B65 2015
  133.1—dc23   2014007820

Speech and thought bubbles in blue are direct quotations from eyewitness accounts.

Design Elements
Shutterstock: alanadesign, Mika Shysh

Designer
Ted Williams

Production Specialist
Laura Manthe

Art Director
Nathan Gassman

Editor
Anthony Wacholtz

Printed in the United States of America in Stevens Point, Wisconsin.
032014   008092WZF14

TABLE OF CONTENTS

*Stories in this book are taken from eyewitness
accounts and cannot be proven true or false.

Legends of haunted places and ghost sightings build excitement and fear in people around the world. Ghost hunters chase these tales, hoping for a viral video, a gripping story, or a personal encounter. The idea of being haunted can be a fascinating and frightening experience for even the bravest ghost hunter.

Being haunted can mean a number of things. It could mean that a ghost of a friend or family member lingers nearby. Some stories tell of apparitions that give warnings before a tragedy or offer help in some way.

A haunting can also be the presence of an evil or mischievous spirit or poltergeist. The spirit may cause destruction or violence. Sometimes these spirits are said to haunt a specific area or location. Other times they may target a single family or person. Tales of people chased from their homes by angry spirits are common in the paranormal world.

Even objects can be haunted. Dolls, cars, or machines are items commonly reported to be haunted.

Many haunted places are thought to have some kind of meaning to the ghosts left behind. Some places, such as theaters or prisons, seem to be natural ghost sites. Other ghosts are attracted to particular families or objects. Nearly half of all Americans believe in ghosts. Almost one quarter say they have seen or been near one.

CAPITOL THEATER HAUNTING

AMITYVILLE HORROR HOUSE

ROBERT THE HAUNTED DOLL

The chilling tales in this book are based off stories told by real people. Flip the page and learn more about these shades of the afterlife. Then decide for yourself if they're fact or fiction.

CHAPTER ONE
THE DUPPY
ROSE HALL, ST, ELIZABETH, JAMAICA, JUNE 2013

A crowd of curious people had been camped out at Desna Hanson's home for days. They had heard of mysterious fires igniting in the home. They hoped to catch a glimpse of the wicked fire poltergeist called a duppy that might be causing them. Vendors sold drinks to the anxiously waiting crowd.

Grab a water while you wait for the duppy!

EEEEEEEKKKKK!!!

Desna Hanson and her family had been terrorized by the duppy since April.

It's back! Oh Lord, it's back!

It caught fire on its own—just like before.

Something strange is happening here. I just can't tell how or where these fires started.

6

Then other mysterious events happened within the house. Stones began to fall inside the home. Objects flew through the house, hitting people.

It's like the stones are coming out of the ceiling!

The duppy refused to let Desna's husband bathe. He was attacked every time he entered the bathroom.

One day Desna's daughter heard a window break. Then suddenly the home was engulfed in flames. The family escaped, but the home was completely destroyed.

We need help! ... We can't live like this ...

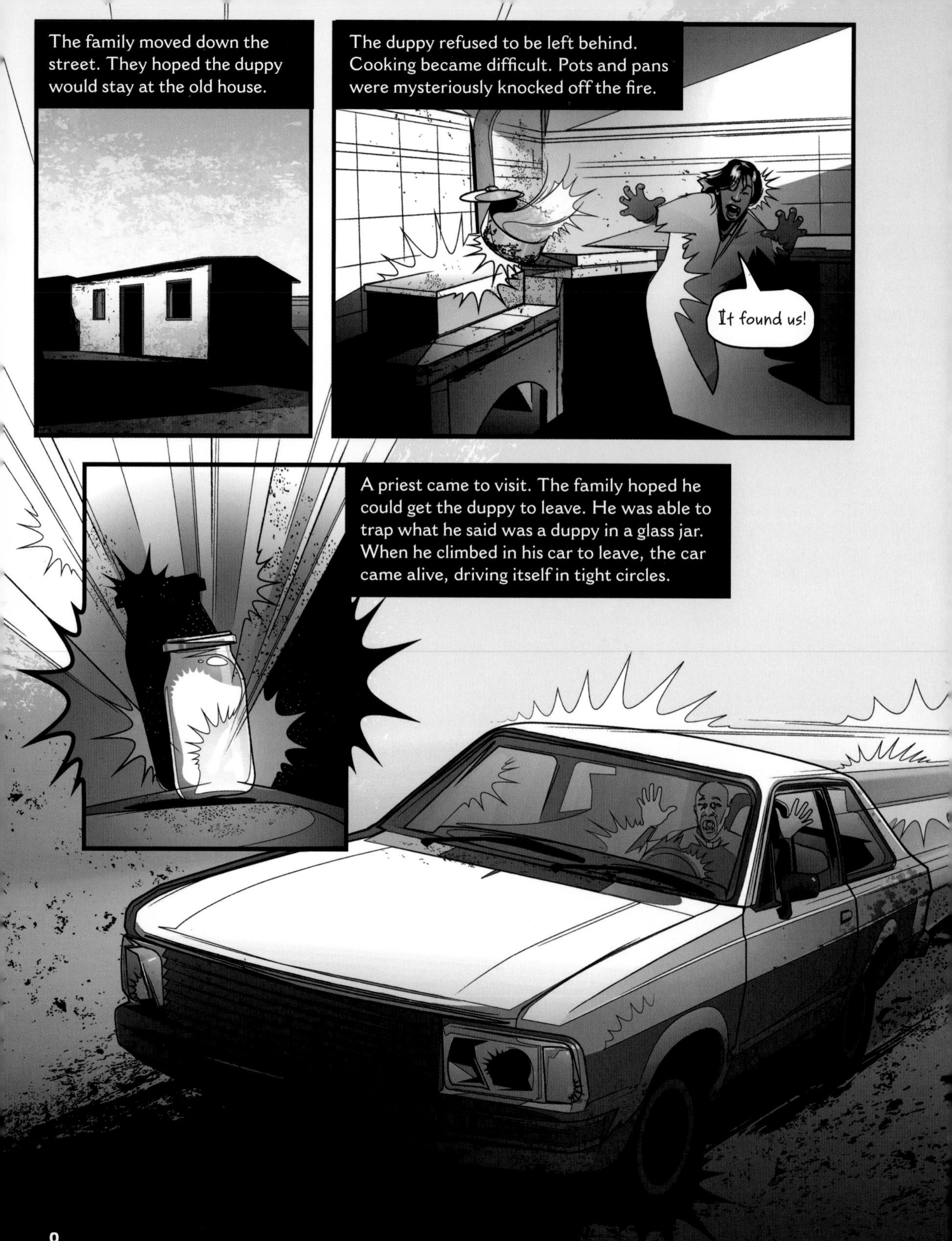
The family moved down the street. They hoped the duppy would stay at the old house.
The duppy refused to be left behind. Cooking became difficult. Pots and pans were mysteriously knocked off the fire.
It found us!
A priest came to visit. The family hoped he could get the duppy to leave. He was able to trap what he said was a duppy in a glass jar. When he climbed in his car to leave, the car came alive, driving itself in tight circles.

The duppy continued to hurl objects around the house.

Are you all right?

I cut myself dodging a rock.

Little did the Hanson family know that the small cut would bring the end to the duppy—and to Desna.

I'm sorry, Desna. We'll have to amputate your foot. Do you have any family you can stay with?

No. We already tried to live with some relatives. They made us leave after their belongings started on fire. I won't bring this duppy into another person's house.

Desna died on July 16, 2013. Her children insist her death was caused by stress from the duppy. The duppy attacks stopped shortly before she died.

YOU DECIDE

The duppy plays a large part in Jamaican folklore. Many people believe the Hansons were being haunted by a fire poltergeist. Other people are suspicious and think the Hansons wanted insurance money. The family claimed the duppy caused more than $15 million Jamaican dollars ($145,000 U.S. dollars) in damage.

CHAPTER TWO

DARK DUDLEYTOWN
DUDLEYTOWN, CONNECTICUT, 1892

John Brophy and his family moved to Dudleytown with the hopes of starting a new life. Dudleytown was sometimes called Owlsbury because of the unusual owls that could be seen all day long.

I've heard this road is called Dark Entry. Entry to what, I wonder?

Come on, John! Let's get unpacked.

Rumor had it that the Brophy children disappeared into the forest.

John Brophy's wife died soon after the move. But that wasn't the last tragedy Brophy would experience.

Boys? Boys?

Villagers began to notice odd behavior from Brophy. People started avoiding him when they saw him coming.

Demons. Demons. They're there. Hooved feet. Dark shapes. Demons.

Before long Brophy's odd behavior took a turn for the worse. Witnesses claimed he set fire to his own house. Then he wandered into the woods … never to be seen again.

YOU DECIDE

Many people in Dudleytown never saw anything strange. Some say that John Brophy is a made-up man in a made-up story. But others claim that Dudleytown is haunted. Visitors to the ghost town have been attacked by unseen spirits, felt chills, and heard disturbing sounds. Strange illnesses and deaths, including insanity and being struck by lightning, have been tied to the town's history.

CHAPTER THREE
HAUNTED HAZEL RIDGE
HAZEL RIDGE CEMETERY, CHARITON COUNTY, MISSOURI, MID 2000s

Ghost hunter Ryan Straub thought
Hazel Ridge Cemetery would be
like any other "haunted" graveyard.
Fellow ghost hunter Kurt Ostrom
couldn't wait to prove him wrong.

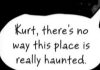

Kurt, there's no
way this place is
really haunted.

I saw a couple of
gravestones shift
last time.

Kurt, can you grab me
a hammer? Kurt? Ah,
never mind, I'll get it.

Kurt, did you take
the tent down?

YOU DECIDE

Some experts believe Hazel Ridge Cemetery is a gateway to another world. Others are skeptical, wondering if Straub and Ostrom correctly mapped out the cemetery's layout. However, Straub has said, "I've been to that place 500 times and every time it's different ... The tombstones moved ... I've got every section mapped out and they're not the way they were."

CHAPTER FOUR

ROBERT THE HAUNTED DOLL

KEY WEST, FLORIDA, LATE 1930s

Anne Otto thought she had married the man of her dreams. What she didn't know was that someone else had a claim on her husband, Gene.

Hey, look! It's my old doll, Robert! It's like he was waiting for me!

When Robert "Gene" Otto was 10 years old, he was given a doll as a gift. He named his new best friend Robert, after himself. Gene was never without Robert. Soon, though, people began to notice some strange behaviors.

Robert, you're not supposed to be doing that! Stop it!

Make me.

Gene grew up and got married, leaving Robert behind. But after the death of Gene's parents, he and Anne moved back to his childhood home.

Robert did it!

I haven't seen this doll in years!

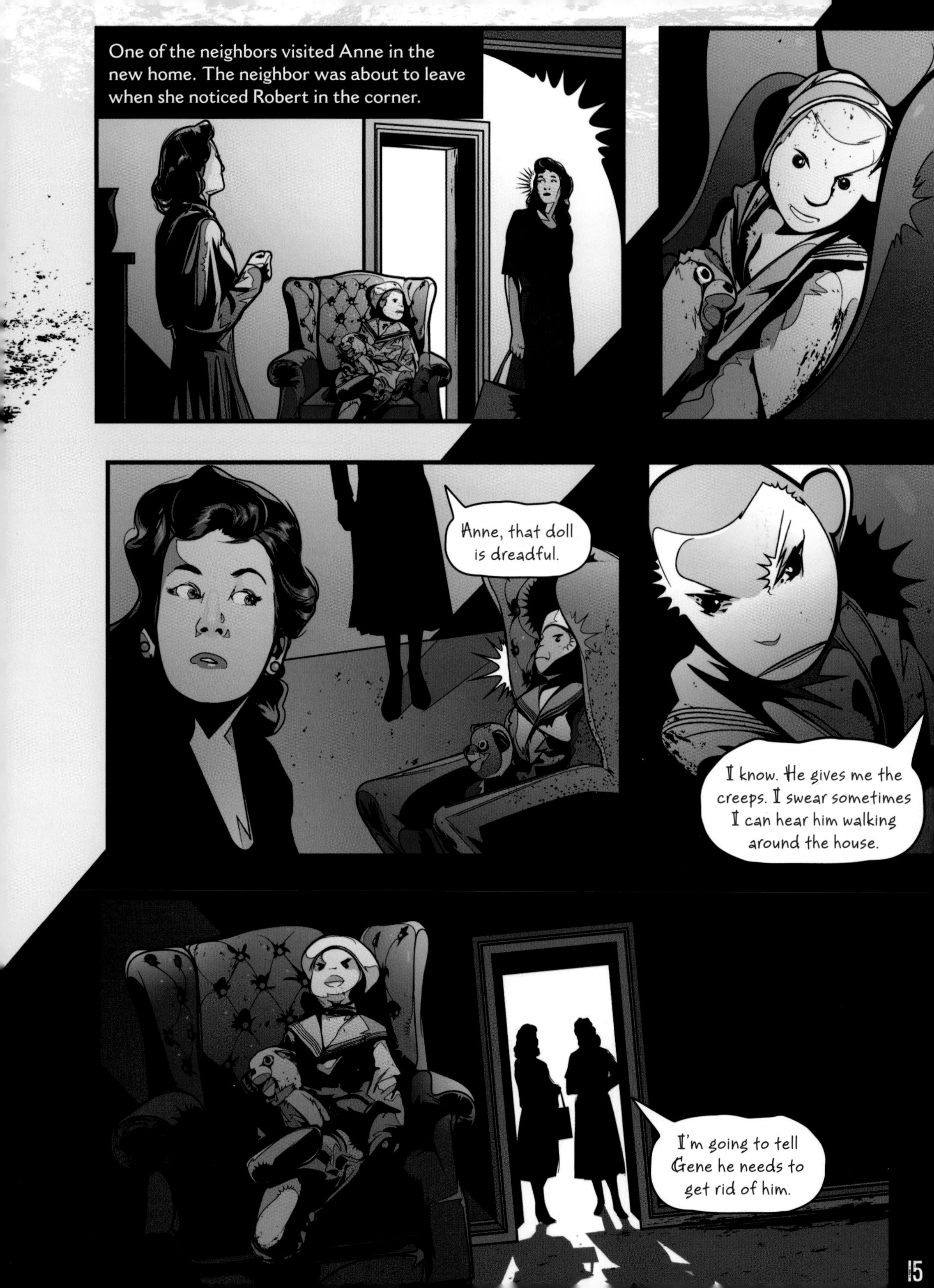
One of the neighbors visited Anne in the new home. The neighbor was about to leave when she noticed Robert in the corner.
Anne, that doll is dreadful.
I know. He gives me the creeps. I swear sometimes I can hear him walking around the house.
I'm going to tell Gene he needs to get rid of him.

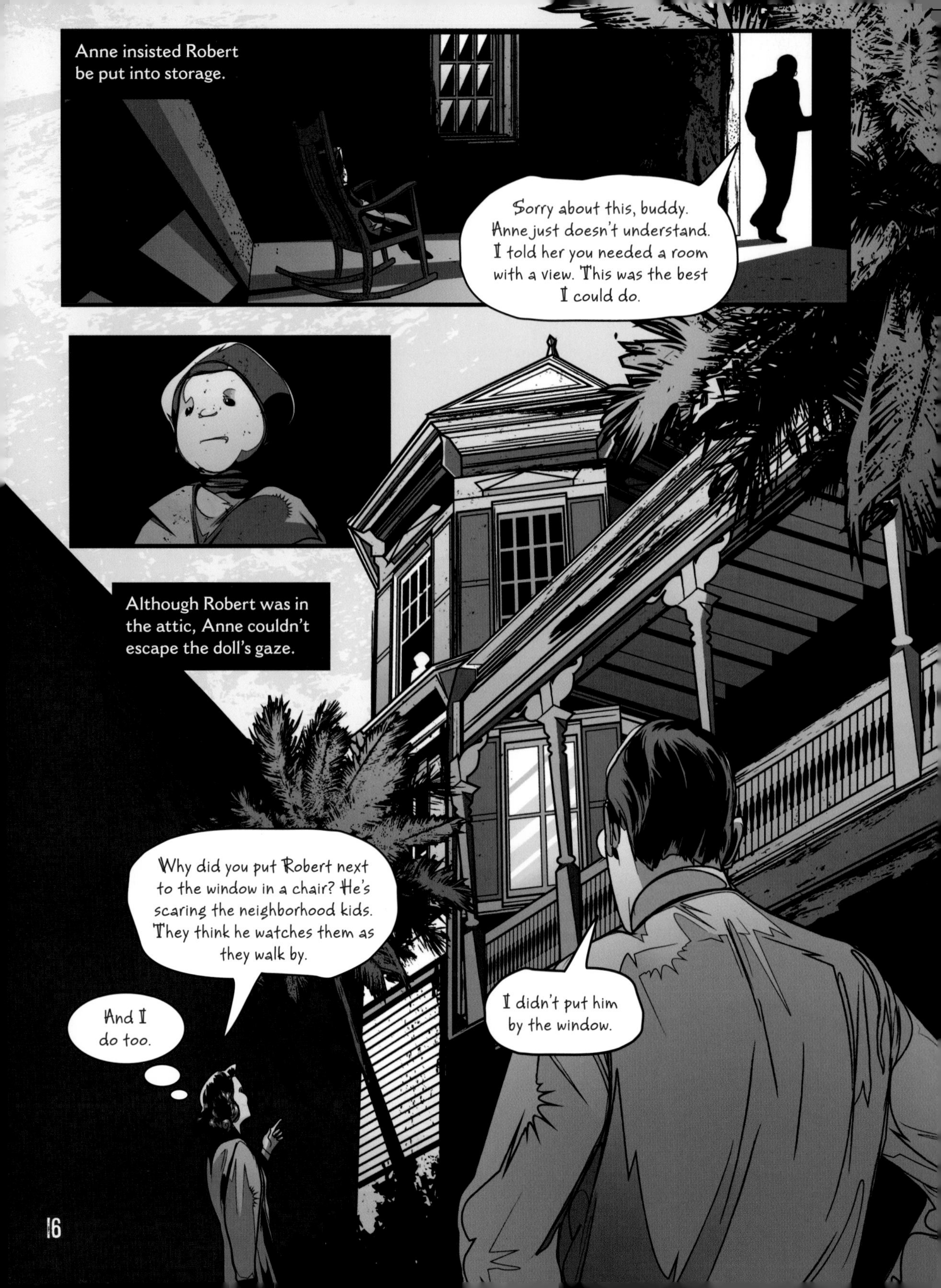
Anne insisted Robert be put into storage.
Sorry about this, buddy. Anne just doesn't understand. I told her you needed a room with a view. This was the best I could do.
Although Robert was in the attic, Anne couldn't escape the doll's gaze.
Why did you put Robert next to the window in a chair? He's scaring the neighborhood kids. They think he watches them as they walk by.
And I do too.
I didn't put him by the window.

Eventually Gene and Anne moved away, leaving Robert behind.

Angry, the doll took his rage out on the new homeowner's daughter.

The doll's alive! It tried to kill me!

Even after the girl's family got rid of the doll, his presence was felt. Legend says that Anne returned to the house after Gene's death. She stood guard in the attic, waiting in case the doll ever returned.

YOU DECIDE

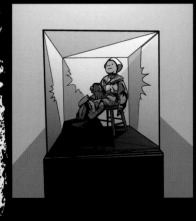

Today Robert the Doll is in a museum in Key West, Florida. Although some visitors don't believe in Robert's haunted story, employees insist that Robert plays pranks on them and moves around the museum. Visitors must ask the doll for permission before taking pictures. Those who forget to ask find their cameras suddenly stop working or end up with blurry photos.

CHAPTER FIVE
THE AMITYVILLE HORROR HOUSE
AMITYVILLE, NEW YORK, DECEMBER 1975

The Amityville Horror House is one of the most well-known poltergeist locations. In 1975 George and Kathy Lutz moved into the house with their three kids, Christopher, Missy, and Daniel.

The family was excited to move into their new home. But they didn't know the house had a dark past. Thirteen months before, a man named Ronald DeFeo Jr. had shot his parents and four siblings in the house.

Who would have guessed that we would be moving into a house like this?

Since then, the house seemed to be a place of evil.

I don't know, but I'm freezing. Aren't you cold?

Ugh! What's that smell?

Mom! Dad! Come see this!

That's disgusting! What is that?

But stink, slime, and cold spots were the least of the Lutzes' problems.

Nighttime was not a time of peace at the Lutz house.

GEORGE!

George, grab me!

George was able to pull Kathy down. Sleep didn't come easy after that.

The Lutzes never knew what surprises the house would bring next.

Quick, open the windows!

In a moment, the flies vanished. It was as though they had never been there at all.

Missy claimed to have made a new friend in the house.

Jodie wants to come in.

Jodie?

Her imaginary friend.

Jodie isn't imaginary!

She lives in my room.

She went outside, and now she wants to come in.

YOU DECIDE

After only three weeks, the Lutzes fled the house and never returned. Some say they couldn't afford the house but didn't want to admit it. A poltergeist was the perfect excuse to leave. DeFeo's lawyer even said he helped the Lutzes make up the story. But in March 2013 Daniel Lutz spoke up. He believed that the events were caused by his father George, who was interested in magic and Spiritualism.

CHAPTER SIX

THE CAPITOL THEATER

CAPITOL THEATER, SALT LAKE CITY, UTAH, LATE 2012

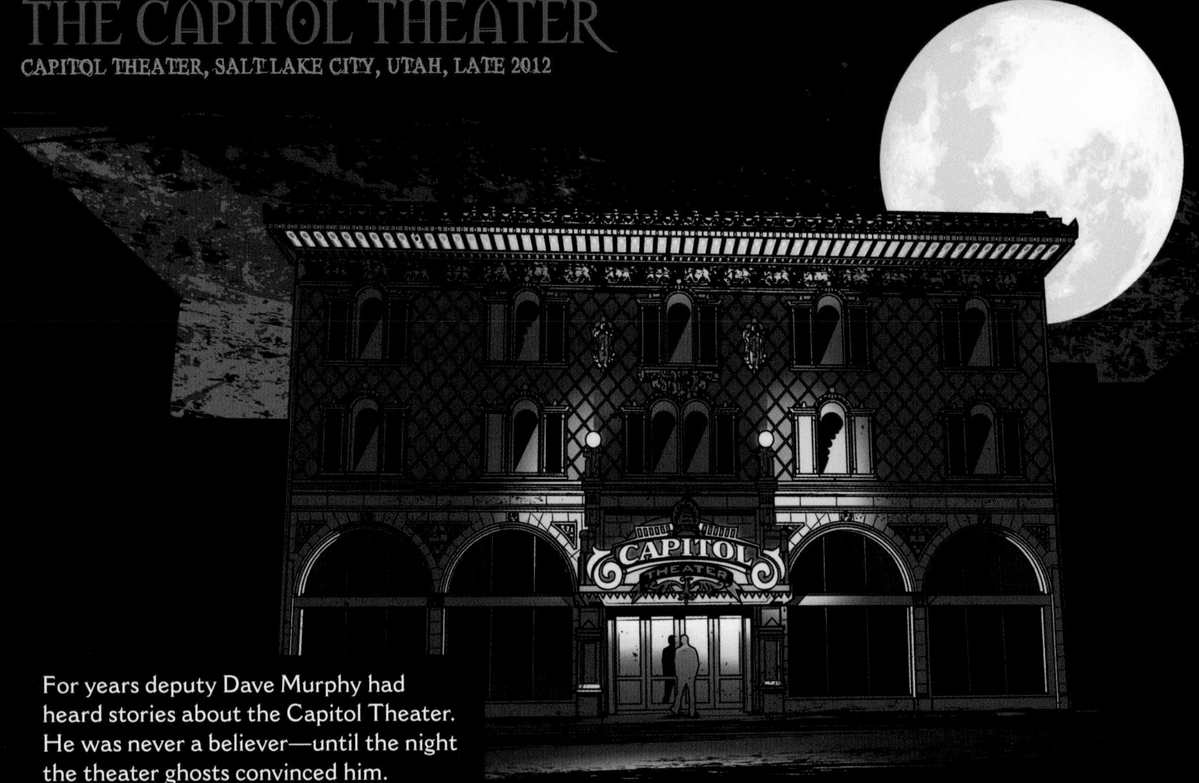

CAPITOL
THEATER

For years deputy Dave Murphy had heard stories about the Capitol Theater. He was never a believer—until the night the theater ghosts convinced him.

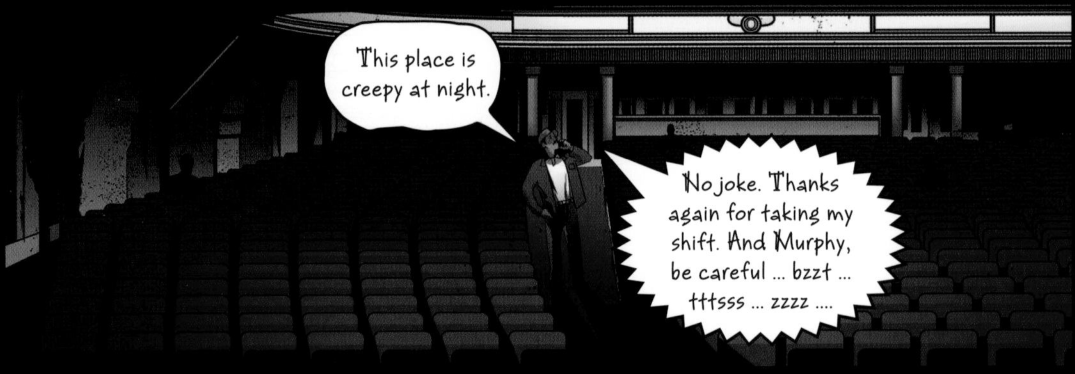

This place is creepy at night.
No joke. Thanks again for taking my shift. And Murphy, be careful ... bzzt ... tttsss ... zzzz ....

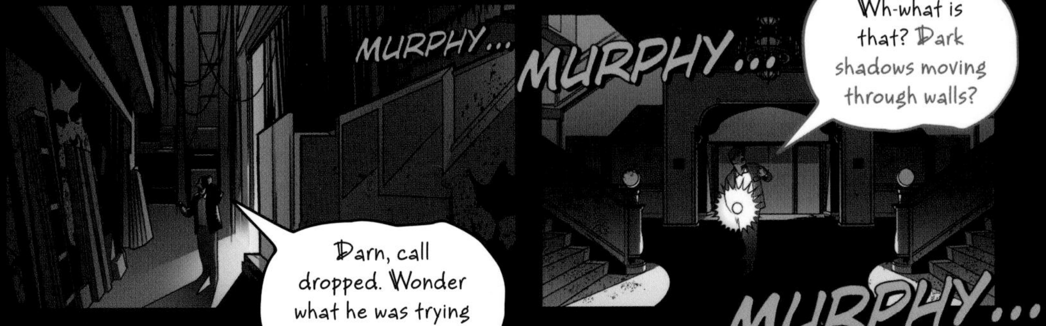

MURPHY...
Darn, call dropped. Wonder what he was trying to warn me about?
MURPHY...
Wh-what is that? Dark shadows moving through walls?
MURPHY...

Terrified of the voices, Murphy tried to escape in the elevator.

Go, go, go ...

DING!

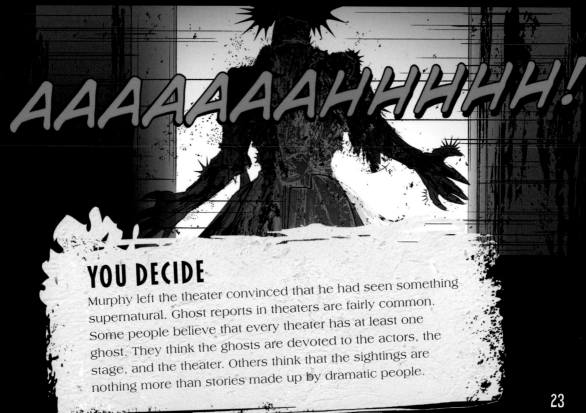

AAAAAAAHHHHHH!

YOU DECIDE

Murphy left the theater convinced that he had seen something supernatural. Ghost reports in theaters are fairly common. Some people believe that every theater has at least one ghost. They think the ghosts are devoted to the actors, the stage, and the theater. Others think that the sightings are nothing more than stories made up by dramatic people.

CHAPTER SEVEN
THE HAMPTON-LILLIBRIDGE HOUSE
SAVANNAH, GEORGIA, 1963

The men said part of the roof collapsed, Mr. Williams. One poor fellow was unlucky enough to fall through.

The Hampton-Lillibridge House has been called the most haunted house in the United States. Investor Jim Williams bought the house as a fix-it-upper. He had the house moved four blocks from its original location to a property he owned.

Shame. Well, the house is moved, at least. Let's get back to work.

He doesn't care about us at all.

Strange things began to happen after the worker's death. Workers reported missing or moved tools and equipment. Laughter and footsteps were heard throughout the house.

SCRITCH SCRITCH SCRITCH

HAHAHA!!!

TAP-TAP-TAP

It sounds like folks having a party upstairs.

But no one else is supposed to be here.

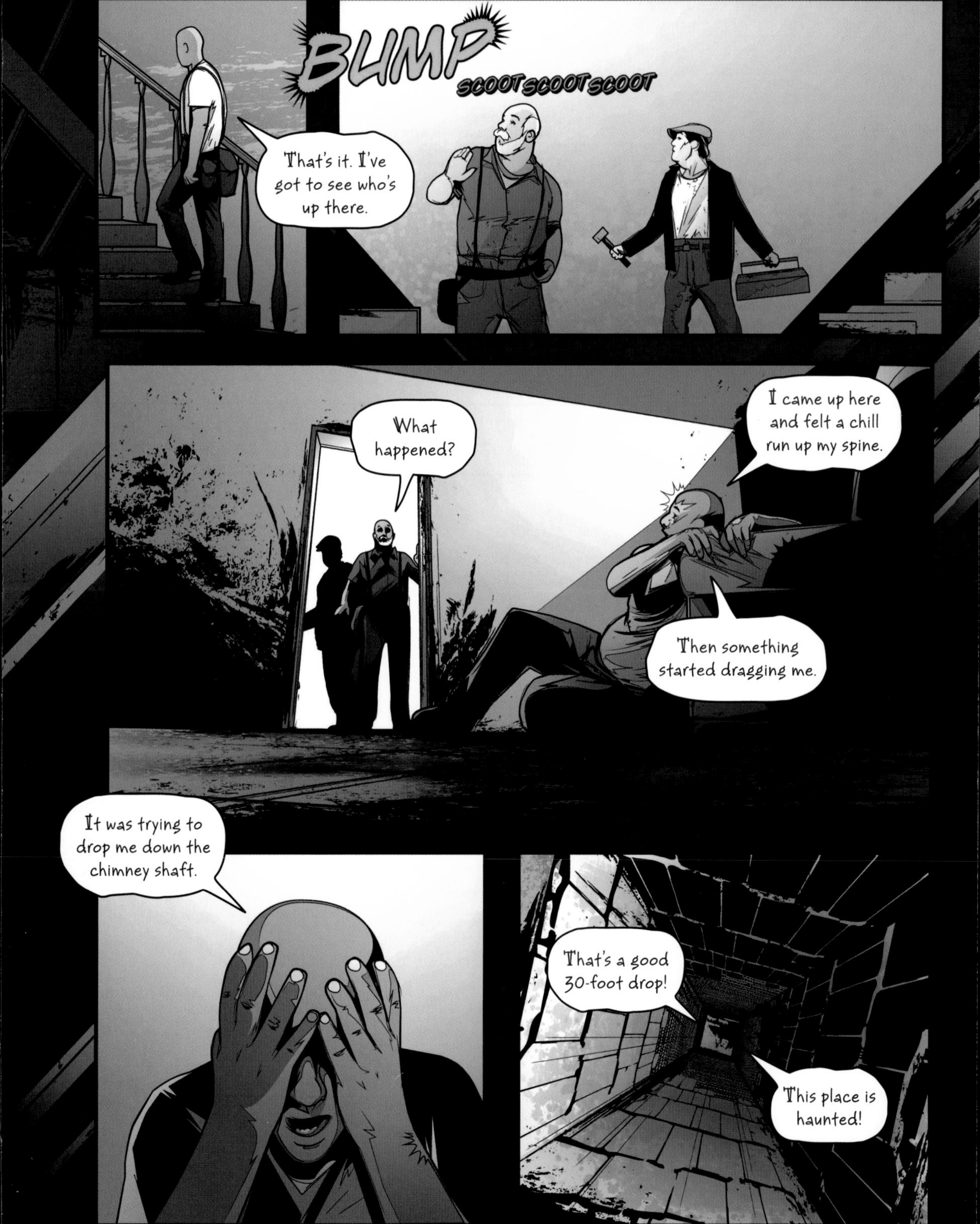
BUMP
SCOOT SCOOT SCOOT
That's it. I've got to see who's up there.
What happened?
I came up here and felt a chill run up my spine.
Then something started dragging me.
It was trying to drop me down the chimney shaft.
That's a good 30-foot drop!
This place is haunted!

Williams did not believe the stories. He even decided to live in the house for a while. But there was only so much he could ignore.

SHIVER!

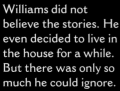

What is it?

I don't know. I feel like there's someone watching me. Let's move inside.

There! Do you see?

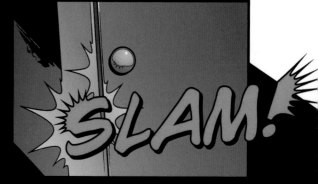

SLAM!

The door is locked!

SCRITCH SCRITCH SCRITCH

HAHAHA!!!

Can you hear that?

Sounds like a party upstairs!

The noises continued above their heads, no matter which floor they were on.

They're on the third floor!

They're on the roof!

There's nowhere to go from there!

How did they get past us?

Okay. I'll admit it. There's something odd about this place!

HAAA...HAAA...HAAA...

YOU DECIDE

A crypt was found when the house was moved. In a rush, Williams told his workers to cover it up. Some say there were skeletons buried there. The hauntings were all reported in 1963. Williams later sold the house. The owners today say they have never witnessed any hauntings.

CHAPTER EIGHT
EASTERN STATE PENITENTIARY
EASTERN STATE PENITENTIARY, PHILADELPHIA, PENNSYLVANIA

Eastern State Penitentiary opened in 1829. Throughout its nearly 190-year history, the prison was the site of many frightening events. Two guards and an unknown number of prisoners were killed there. Hundreds more died of disease or old age.

Nearly 60 paranormal teams visit the prison every year. They have reported many strange and unusual events. The following story represents a collection of reports about the ominous penitentiary.

Do you think we'll see the ghost dog?

Who, Pep? Forget that—I want to hear Al Capone!

Ghost hunters use various equipment to capture supernatural encounters. They record movements with video cameras and try to catch EVP with audio devices. Some hunters use trigger objects, such as a Bible, that might encourage ghosts to make themselves known.

HMMPH!

Did you hear that? Stay here while I check it out.

Strange noises are only some of the unusual occurrences at Eastern State. People have seen shadowy figures and tortured faces. Wails have been heard throughout the prison.

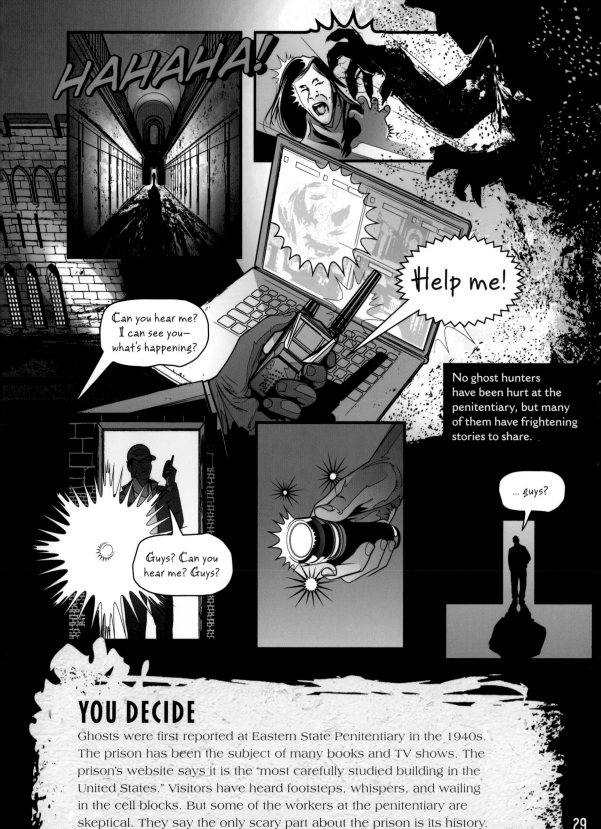

YOU DECIDE

Ghosts were first reported at Eastern State Penitentiary in the 1940s. The prison has been the subject of many books and TV shows. The prison's website says it is the "most carefully studied building in the United States." Visitors have heard footsteps, whispers, and wailing in the cell blocks. But some of the workers at the penitentiary are skeptical. They say the only scary part about the prison is its history.

GLOSSARY

apparition (ap-uh-RISH-uhn)—the visible appearance of a ghost

crypt (KRIPT)—a chamber used as a grave

EVP—sounds or voices heard during electronic recordings that can't be explained; EVP stands for electronic voice phenomenon

haunt (HAWNT)—to cause unexplained events to occur or appear as a ghost in a certain place

ominous (OM-uh-nuhss)—describes something that gives the impression that something bad is going to happen

paranormal (pair-uh-NOR-muhl)—having to do with an unexplained event that has no scientific explanation

penitentiary (PEN-uh-ten-shee-air-ee)—a state or federal prison in the United States

poltergeist (POLE-tuhr-gyst)—a noisy ghost

Spiritualism (SPIHR-uh-choo-uh-li-zuhm)—a religion based on the belief that people can speak to the spirits of the dead

trigger object (TRIG-uhr OB-jekt)—an object used to attract ghosts; trigger objects are usually items the ghost may recognize, such as stuffed animals or photographs

READ MORE

Bingham, Jane. *Ghosts and Haunted Houses.* Solving Mysteries with Science. Chicago: Raintree, 2014.

Hamilton, S. L. *Ghost Hunting.* Xtreme Adventure. Minneapolis: ABDO Pub. Co., 2014.

Lunis, Natalie. *Tragic Theaters.* Scary Places. New York: Bearport Publishing, 2014.

INTERNET SITES

FactHound offers a safe, fun way to find Internet sites related to this book. All sites on FactHound have been researched by our staff.

Here's all you do:

Visit *www.facthound.com*

Type in this code: 9781491402450

Check out projects, games and lots more at
www.capstonekids.com

INDEX